Baseline Breathing

The Enigma of Optimal Breathing

Derik Glick

Contents

Introduction

We live in extremely stressed-filled environments. They can lead us to be stuck in fight or flight states. It is well known that these prolonged states of stress cause unease—or dis-ease—in the body. But, what if there was a way to help our bodies adapt to these ever-changing stress levels? There is. Breathwork hacks our autonomic nervous system. Its slow, rhythmic breathing can regulate our heart rate and nervous system while simultaneously sending chemical signals to the brain to reduce stress levels.

Like a warm embrace in the midst of a tumultuous storm, breathwork is an effective tool to help you navigate life's difficult times and reduce stress, worry, and frustration. Much like a hug can help soothe your worries away, breathwork calms the body and mind, helping you reconnect with yourself and feel more relaxed and centered. It enables the body to shift from fight or flight to rest and digest mode, which is where optimal brain functioning occurs. We go from sending cortisol to sending oxytocin to the brain, and this is just the beginning of the benefits. With just breathwork, we promote increased blood oxygenation, better digestion, decreased inflammation, increased healing, and much more.

This book is about self-empowerment and having more control of the body through breathing techniques that you can do without anyone else coaching you when things get tough. The way you breathe can profoundly influence the performance of every cell in your body. Functional breathwork is a level-up of every function of the body. By engaging in it, you are enabling each and every part of yourself to reach its peak level of functioning. So, when someone asks how important the understanding and implementation of optimal breathing is to the body, there is nothing that rivals it. Its potential to facilitate change in the body is second to none. Therefore, when I was first taught how to use breathing to empower my health, I couldn't really fathom the benefits.

A short list of the initial benefits of optimal breathing I felt is as follows; increased energy throughout the day, better sleep, increased stress management, and lower body fat percentage. After I put it into practice for 6 months, it started to affect almost everything in my life. I enjoyed benefits that I wouldn't have believed were right in front of me unless I had the first-hand experience. This goes to show how unaware you can be of what is truly beneficial and important. Apparently, what I didn't know was limiting my health, peace, and happiness.

Getting to my current level of knowledge, and being able to apply it, took me almost 20 years and involved much trial and error. My journey has led me to many places and through many experiences. I have attended hundreds of weekend retreats, spent thousands of hours researching breathing studies and health books, visited health retreats across the globe, received training from Wim Hof teachers and Holotropic trainers, as well as trained as an advanced instructor with Oxygen Advantage, plus had some personal coaching along the way. I then applied what I learned for the benefit of as many people as I could. I eventually built a non-profit to raise awareness by offering free books, consultations, and seminars to veterans and first responders. I never imagined finding such rewarding work. It is my hope that with this book you will find all of the benefits that myself and others have, if not more.

The mission of this book is to help others understand this information, then create and implement the habits that will bring about the fastest progression toward ideal health, both mental and physical. I will provide a great deal of scientific data, reliable techniques and practices, studies, and books to help you continue your exploration of optimal breathing. Many of the studies are on my website, in order to keep the book more concise, but I would implore you to look into them.

This book is the culmination of all I have learned, and is intended to be your unbreakable breathing foundation. It is an art of balance to distill such a wealth of complex and in-depth concepts of the body without leaving out important information. Inevitably, these concepts had to be simplified to some extent to allow for quicker application by a greater audience. With that said, the concepts remain incredibly deep and hopefully their outlines here will serve as your starting point to delve deeper into how your body functions and the science behind it.

Journey on.

Chapter 1
The Benefits of Optimal Breathing

enefits from breathwork experienced by me are exclusive to me, and I frequently receive feedback from others who have experiences that differ. This is a very personal journey that involves your own strengths and weaknesses. Therefore benefits will vary from person to person. I would suggest remaining open-minded about your breath and its potential to create change. Two of my favorite quotes that I commonly use to express the gravity of breathwork are

"You don't what you don't know"

and

"You're only as strong as your weakest link."

These two quotes are essential to understanding the power of breathwork and what it can mean for your life. Exactly what it will mean for you depends heavily on the level of commitment you put in, as well as how much effort is made to understand the science behind it.

Benefits of Optimal Breathing

The benefits I personally experienced were beyond anything I could have imagined, but some of the feedback that I've received is as follows:

- Improved mental and physical performance
- Improved sleep
- Improved concentration
- Increased calmness
- Less coughing
- Fewer asthma symptoms (including wheezing or nasal congestion)
- Fewer cavities and better overall mouth health (less time with the dentist)
- Improved sports performance
- Improved energy
- Helps avoid bad breath
- Ensures normal facial development and straight teeth
- 10-20% greater oxygenation of blood
- Better memory recall
- Aided in body detox
- Increased VO2 Max (how much oxygen the body can use, calculated by weight)
- Fewer headaches
- Decreased lower back pain
- Better digestion
- Better lymphatic function

Since there are such benefits that come with optimal breathing, there are also issues that can arise from dysfunctional breathing. The main issue? Decreased blood oxygenation. This can cause a cascade of issues such as cellular dysfunction and decreased immune response. It also increases the likelihood of other illnesses like depression, anxiety, sleep disorders, chronic fatigue syndrome, and so much more, examples of which will be shown throughout the next chapters.

The health benefits of breathwork are numerous and far-reaching. It affects all aspects of the body, from boosting energy levels to improving focus, sleep, and relaxation. As we explore the different breathing techniques in this book, you will learn how to use them during times of anxiety, worry, and frustration for improved mental well-being and performance. But before we embark on that journey, we need to take the first step of the ladder - self examination.

The Need for Self Examination

Socrates' sage advice, "A life unexamined is not worth living," reminds us of the importance of introspection and reflection.

I can't stress enough the importance of self-examination or self-reflection to all areas of life, but I think it may be the most rewarding when it comes to our breath. I understand that I might be a little biased here... because of the focus of my research for the last decade or so... still, this is your opportunity to take stock of where you are with your breathing right now.

For that purpose, I have made a list of common breathing problems. The idea is to address our baseline and identify what we'd like to change or improve. Any issues you're dealing with are to be noted, using the scaling system to gauge their severity.

Writing with complete honesty is an incredibly powerful tool; it can help us become aware of our own thoughts and feelings, and ultimately lead to a more positive life. Nobody is going to look at this other than you, so be open and honest about your mental or physical health and what you would like to improve or have issues with. You will be able to look back and compare after you implement some new breathing habits.

Many of us will experience a variety of symptoms listed below as a result of dysfunctional breathing. Ask yourself - do any of the symptoms below arise in my life? To get an understanding of how often these issues arise, we can give them a severity rating. Do this on a scale from 0 to 10, with 0 representing that it never occurs and 10 that it happens all the time. This can help identify areas where we need to work on improving our breathing habits and overall well-being.

The checklist for the symptoms can look like this:

- Daytime sleepiness
- High-stress levels during the day
- Overwhelming stress or anxiety during the day
- Hard to change mental state fairly quickly and consistently
- Experiencing cold hands or feet
- Yawning regularly during the day
- Breathing through your mouth during the day/night
- Waking up with a dry mouth
- Brain Fog
- History of dental issues
- Speech impediments
- Frequent urination at night
- Coughing
- Excessive sweating
- Wheezing
- Exercise-induced mild asthma
- Frequent colds
- Achy muscles
- Breathlessness at rest
- Frequent sighs
- Insomnia/broken sleep
- Frequent yawning
- Poor concentration or academic performance

- Snoring
- Headaches
- Bad breath
- Lower back pain

For most of us, breathing is pretty much in automatic or autopilot mode. Although we may take control of our breath every now and then, it is hard to do better than the natural flow that comes with breathing automatically. Most of us are stuck with just a few breathing tools. We may have been told to simply 'take deeper breaths', but still find ourselves short of breath at the end. Our society as a whole tends to breathe more aggressively, which is counterintuitive if you consider the current research and science.

Dysfunctional breathing is not just breathing too much or too little. Much of dysfunctional breathing stems from a lack of understanding and the common misconceptions that we use to form our breathing behaviors. Chapters 2 & 3 contain crucial information that debunks common misconceptions about breathing and will help you to understand its impact and consequences. For example, many studies have revealed the substantial effects of mouth versus nasal breathing on lung health and the amount of oxygen that enters our body – highlighting the importance of developing healthy respiratory habits.

Autopilot systems can always be upgraded. We can learn to take control of our breath when needed. Our current breathing autopilot modes are designed by our education, genetics, past and current environmental conditioning, and much more. This includes everything from past traumas and mental states, to chemical exposures, and so much more. We can't be certain of everything that contributes to it. But we can be certain of one thing, which is that you don't need to have a stress-free life to have great breathing.

The Impact of Being Able To Adapt

We live in an ever-expanding, multifaceted, stressed-filled environment that can lead us to get stuck in fight-or-flight. There are even A.I. programs that create marketing which is engineered to elicit an emotional response and is customized to you! So, on top of life's normal stress, we have smart computers and phones that jack up our stress responses exponentially. We also know that prolonged states of stress cause unease, or dis-ease, in the body.

That's where breathwork comes in handy. It can tap into the body's nervous system and override the fight-or-flight response that otherwise keeps us in a state of chronic tension and stress. As we practice slow and conscious breathing, signals are sent to our brain causing it to relax and shift into rest and digest mode. This allows us to move from releasing cortisol—the stress hormone—to releasing oxytocin, the feel-good hormone. The benefits of breathwork include increased oxygen circulation in our bodies, improved digestion, decreased inflammation, and enhanced brain function. This all adds up to an environment more conducive to healing.

The outcome of breathing, just like any tool, depends on how it is used. It can be used for personal growth and better health... or pain and self-destruction. The benefit of being aware of the breath and its relationship to our physical, mental, and emotional state is that it can help us become more adaptive to life's ever-changing environment. When we can recognize the signs that our body is getting stuck in fight-or-flight, and take steps to move into a relaxation response with breathwork, then we can be more resilient and better equipped to handle whatever comes our way.

Be warned - the ability to fully apply these breathing styles, techniques, and habits is not one that develops overnight. While there is an immediate reward for much of this breathwork, the compounding effect over time is where the real magic happens. It doesn't cost any money for most of these changes, just time, and the benefits are exponential for both our short and long-term health.

I have included many studies from past and current scientists and their analyses of them for reference. In keeping with the mission of Baseline Breathing, I will try to explain the concepts in a way that can be understood and shared with any age group. I think the most important part of receiving knowledge is applying it to yourself, but coming a close second is being able to share it with those who might need it. Understanding and demonstrating by example our breathwork in our daily lives is very important, especially if we want to effectively share this information.

Therefore, I believe it is absolutely important to focus on our own application of breathwork before we share new information. I would rather not rush into an explanation that is hard to understand. So, make sure you spend the time to understand and practice the information you are about to receive.

You can share this information with anyone you want, but it will be even more impactful if they see the differences in you and come to ask what has changed or how they too can manage stress. After observing your transformation, people are more likely to seek advice from you. They will be more responsive to new information and more likely to implement it. So my message is to be a living, breathing example of optimal breathwork! It will have a ripple effect in your environment that will be quite noticeable.

We all have the capacity to create a uniquely tailored balance to bring about our optimal health and performance. Finding this balance requires patience and practice, but in the end, the rewards are exponential and compounding. Achieving your own ideal of balance and harmony is one of the greatest gifts you can give yourself.

Your goal is to become your own breathing director. As your own breathing director, your job is to get the most out of the respiratory system and find the best balance to optimize your chances of achieving your current goals. Whether you are preparing for a public speech, for sleeping, for putting your body under stress, or for working out intensely you will need to adjust your breathing style. Your cells will need more oxygen to remove excess carbon dioxide (CO_2). In different situations, your body will have different needs. These needs will be easy to understand with practice and understanding of your role as breathing director. Let's dispel some myths and misconceptions.

Chapter 2
A Historical Perspective
Discovering the Study of Breathwork in the Western World

Studying breathwork has been a part of human culture for centuries, if not millennia. For over two hundred years of western world history, the study of breath control and its effects on health have been documented by various experts in the field. This is a very exclusionary, western cultural approach; it doesn't include Pranayama or other eastern practices that have been applied to control breathing over the millennia.

These are just a few of the many researchers who have dedicated their lives to studying breathwork and its effects on health. Over two hundred years of western world history has seen an incredible amount of research into how controlling your breath can improve your overall well-being, and the evidence is continually growing.

The history of the evolution of breathing has shown us that breathing is more than just a physical act, it has the power to affect both our mental and physical health. By understanding the history of those who have come before us and applying the advice they left behind, we can take control of our breath and use it to improve our lives. Anyhow, let's talk of breathwork's evolution in western history:

George Catlin (1796 – 1872)

He wrote the book *'Shut Your Mouth Save Your Life'*

George Catlin first published his book in 1869, and you may know of him by his art of the Western frontier. He started out as a lawyer in Philadelphia, but became disillusioned with high society and with his failing health, he wanted a change. He was a well-known portrait painter that became set on breaking out and going into nature.

So, he packed and prepared to journey west. He ended up spending time with over 50 Native American tribes, creating many infamous paintings along the way. He would spend much of his time living with the tribes and learning about their cultures, painting over 600 portraits and taking hundreds of pages of notes. Many of the tribes had very little exposure to Europeans, and were very much unaffected by them at that time. One of the things he noticed was their overall vigorous health, straight teeth, and limited health problems.

He believed that their vibrant health was due to the way they lived, which revolved around physical activity and optimal breathing. Their approach to healing was quite different to western practices. The tribes believed that breathing through the mouth deformed the face, weakened the body, and increased stress and disease. Moreover, breathing through the nose keeps you strong, healthy, and promotes a more functional face. The practice of closing a baby's mouth with their fingers after feeding or while they were sleeping was common practice in the tribes. Catlin also summarized that adult tribe members would not smile with their mouths open, in keeping with the importance of nasal-only breathing.

He was so intrigued, that at the age of 56—20 years after his western exploration—he decided to explore South America. He wanted to see if this "breathing medicine" was used by those tribes as well. Following 7 years of traversing the Andes, from Argentina to Brazil, he discerned that all tribes shared similar breathing beliefs.

His book is a short and easy read on the benefits of nasal breathing and the perils of mouth breathing. Western medicine had no cure for what he was suffering from, with his doctors suggesting he wouldn't make it to 40, he turned to this style of breathing for health and a possible remedy. Desperate for a solution and armed with the knowledge that nasal breathing could help improve health, he made a conscious effort to practice this breathing technique every day. To his surprise, his health improved dramatically after a committed effort to nasal breathing and he lived a full life until his death at age 76. He credited his long life to this ancient healing practice, and often referred to it as, "the breathing medicine".

Dr. Otto Warburg (1883-1970)

He may not have been studying breathwork directly, but his discovery demonstrates how important oxygen is to our body and its functions, thus relating it to breathing. He discovered the cause of cancer in 1923, and the previously unknown functions of cancer cells.

Dr. Otto Warburg was a German biochemist and physician who won the Nobel Prize in Physiology in 1931. He was best known for his discovery that cancer cells have a fundamentally different metabolism than normal cells. In 1923, Warburg discovered that cancer cells primarily produce energy through a process called glycolysis, even in the presence of ample oxygen. This is in contrast to normal cells, which produce energy through a process called cellular respiration when oxygen is available.

He famously stated that "deprive a cell of 35% of its oxygen for 48 hours and it may become cancerous". This observation suggested that a lack of oxygen—entering a state known as hypoxia—may play a role in the development of cancer. Warburg's discovery was a major breakthrough in the field of cancer research, and laid the foundation for our understanding of the metabolic changes that occur in cancer cells.

In addition to his research on the metabolic changes that occur in cancerous cells, Warburg was also a pioneering scientist in the field of cellular respiration. He made numerous contributions to our understanding of the process of cellular respiration and how it is regulated in normal cells. He discovered that cells take up oxygen from their environment and use it to produce energy. This discovery was the first step towards understanding how breathing, and more specifically breathwork, can have an effect on cellular health. His work laid the foundation for the modern study of cellular metabolism and has been widely cited in scientific literature.

Warburg's groundbreaking research still influences the landscape of oncological studies today, with numerous investigators probing the power of targeting malignant cells through metabolism as a possible treatment. The legacy of Dr. Otto Warburg and his discovery of the metabolic differences between cancer and normal cells continues to shape our understanding of the underlying causes of cancer and how it can be treated.

Yandell Henderson (1873 – 1944)

The Importance of CO2 to Bodily Functions

Yandell was directly involved in studying breathing and the related mechanics with different combinations of gasses and environments. Yandell Henderson was a prominent figure in the American medical world, holding positions including being a director of the Yale Laboratory of Applied Physiology at Yale University, and a member of both the National Academy of

Baseline Breathing

Sciences and the American Philosophical Society. Additionally, he served as chairman for the Section on Physiology & Pathology of the prestigious American Medical Association.

As an American physiologist, he was known for his pioneering work in the field of respiratory physiology. He was a respected expert in the study of the function of the respiratory system.

One of Henderson's most famous quotes is that "CO2 is the chief hormone of the entire body". This statement highlights the pivotal role that carbon dioxide plays in regulating our respiratory drive, or the way we control our breathing. Henderson believed that the levels of carbon dioxide in our bodies play a crucial role in determining our respiratory drive and the distribution of oxygen throughout our bodies.

According to Henderson, changes in carbon dioxide levels in the blood can stimulate or inhibit our breathing, which in turn affects the amount of oxygen that is delivered to our tissues and organs. This is an important concept, because a lack of oxygen can lead to a slew of health problems, including heart disease, stroke, and other respiratory disorders. Thus, it is imperative to recognize the correlation between carbon dioxide levels and respiratory drive in order to maintain good health.

Henderson's work continues to be relevant today and has helped shape our understanding of the respiratory system and how it functions. His pioneering research on the role of carbon dioxide in regulating respiratory drive has provided valuable insights into how we can maintain a healthy respiratory system and prevent the development of respiratory diseases. The legacy of Yandell Henderson and his contributions to respiratory physiology will continue to influence the field for years to come.

Dr Buteyko (1923-2003)

Dr. Konstantin Buteyko was a Russian medical doctor whose practice was in attending to severely sick and ill patients. After spending so much time with these patients, he started to recognize a pattern - as patients moved closer to the end of their lives, they would begin to breathe more heavily. He concluded that as their hyperventilation worsened, they were getting closer to the end of their lives.

By 1950, he was made head of the Russian space project in Novosibirsk. This allowed him access to even more equipment and staff to investigate his theories on breathing. By the 1960s he had spent thousands of hours researching and testing his theories, concluding that breathing plays a fundamental role in overall health and many diseases. At that time, he believed over 150 health conditions were related to over-breathing or hyperventilation. This information remained classified for a long time. It was only in the 1990s that Dr. Buteyko and some of his students were able to travel to the west and share his discoveries.

Dr. Buteyko developed a breathing technique that has been used to treat a variety of health conditions, including cancer, asthma, and other serious health issues. He was convinced that this multitude of health issues came about as a result of hyperventilation (taking in more air than the body requires). He argued that this type of breathing leads to a decrease in carbon dioxide levels in the body, which can cause a range of physiological changes and health problems.

Dr. Buteyko's theories have since obtained substantial recognition worldwide and have been validated through intensive research and studies. According to his theory, increasing the levels of carbon dioxide in the body through controlled breathing can help to improve health and overall cell function. This can be achieved through the use of the Buteyko breathing technique, which involves controlled, slow breathing that is designed to reduce the amount of air taken in and increase carbon dioxide levels.

In England, the Buteyko breathing technique has been used to treat asthma and has been found to be effective in reducing the symptoms of the condition. One study conducted in England found that patients who used the Buteyko technique experienced a significant reduction in the frequency and severity of asthma attacks, as well as improved lung function and quality of life. These findings clearly support the idea that the Buteyko breathing technique can have a positive impact on respiratory health.

But the Buteyko breathing technique is not limited to the treatment of cancer and asthma. It has also been used to treat a variety of other health conditions, including sleep apnea, chronic obstructive pulmonary disease (COPD), and stress. In each of these scenarios, the technique has been found to be effective in reducing symptoms and improving overall health and well-being.

Dr. Buteyko's theories, and the associated breathing technique, remain trusted and employed to this day to assist countless individuals in restoring their health and well-being.

Dr. Weston Price (1870-1948)

Dr. Weston Price was a dentist and researcher who conducted extensive studies on the relationship between dental health, facial structure, and overall health. One of his key findings was that the shape and structure of a child's face and dental arches were closely related to their breathing habits, and that any breathing issues or changes in facial features present can worsen over generations. This was noted in Dr. Weston Price's book, but we can also stop and sometimes reverse some progression of mouth breathing. There are many orthodontists now that have kids in braces from very early ages because of how small their mouths are. Nowadays, adults have even more options to open up their airways and better regulate breathing.

From what he gathered from his studies, most of us start out with optimal breathing mechanics. When you watch a newborn or a toddler breathe, they primarily use their nose and breathe deep into the belly. They run around with their Buddha's belly breathing at an optimal level! It's only after the toddler years that most breathing habits start to go off course.

Research studies and the associated health advantages have become increasingly prevalent and acknowledged, so much so that many physicians are beginning to take note. This is great news, but we cannot wait for someone else to bring about improvements for us when it comes to such an important aspect of our overall health. We must be proactive. We must act now to ensure the health of ourselves, our family, and those around us. It is evident that improving our breathing habits can have numerous benefits to our overall well being; from cleansing and purifying our respiratory system, to boosting oxygen levels in our body and optimizing cellular function - a clean bill of health starts with an informed understanding of optimal breathing!

Chapter 3
Breathing Chemistry
Unveiling the Misconceptions of Breathing

Breathing is one of the most basic and essential functions for life, yet many of us don't pay much attention to it. But, if you take a closer look, there's actually a lot of interesting chemistry going on behind the scenes of this seemingly simple process. In this chapter, we'll explore the biochemical mechanics that make breathing possible and learn how oxygen fuels our cells. So, put on your lab coat and get ready to dive into the fascinating world of breathing and the most common misconceptions.

Unchallenged, common knowledge in any area of our life can hurt us. It is our responsibility to continually challenge the prevailing wisdom around us and within our own minds. Either your idea will be proven to have merit, or it will need to be reconsidered. Let's start off with the biggest misconceptions about breathing and work our way down. I believe this chapter might be the most egregious example of the negative effects of common knowledge.

Common Breathing Misconceptions

Partial truths can be dangerous. From the notion that "we only use 10% of our lungs" to believing holding your breath will make you smarter, there are numerous misconceptions when it comes to breathing. I will list these in order of what I believe to be the most harmful to our concept of health, but you can judge for yourself after you read them.

1. "CO2 is just a waste gas, and the more you get rid of it the better."

This is a serious partial truth, as it is leaving out the importance of the function of CO2 in the body. Having the proper levels of CO2 in the lungs is paramount for cellular function and oxygen distribution. But hold on a minute! Yes, I too was once taught that CO2 was a waste gas that was created as a byproduct of respiration. So, when did this knowledge change? One might think it has only recently been uncovered—that was my first thought—but that is false! It was discovered in 1904, by a Danish scientist named Christan Bohr, and was named the Bohr Effect. I have read some literature that states it was discovered in Russia 20 years earlier, but I only have evidence from Christan Bohr.

The Bohr Effect refers to the relationship between CO2 levels and pH levels in our blood, and how this can affect the way oxygen is carried in parts of the blood. Hemoglobin, a protein found in red blood cells, binds to oxygen and helps transport it throughout our bodies. When pH levels are too high, our bodies use CO2 to bring pH back down to optimal functioning levels. This causes hemoglobin in red blood cells to hold on too tightly to oxygen when it is most needed for release into organs, hindering efficient oxygen delivery. This is an example of homeostasis – a process used by organisms to maintain physiological balance in their changing environments. The Bohr

Baseline Breathing

Effect helps us understand how homeostasis works, and explains why maintaining the right balance of CO2 is important when it comes to regulating pH levels for healthy functioning.

So, in optimal breathing function we are looking for the right balance of CO2 - having too much or too little in your body would cause it to not function correctly. The golden balance is CO2 at a partial pressure in the body of 5%. We don't breathe in CO2 from the atmosphere, we build it up in our bodies as a byproduct of cell function. When we exhale too fast, it can lower the CO2 level and have a negative effect on oxygen levels and distribution in the body.

Just like money serves as a medium of exchange and keeps economies running, CO2 is essential for maintaining the balance of our systems. It serves as a regulator, ensuring vital functions like oxygen delivery don't get out of whack. Too much or too little of it, just like too much or too little money in an economy, can cause imbalances.

Furthermore, how I explain this concept to kids is that our body also needs a certain amount of carbon dioxide to make sure that the oxygen gets to where it needs to go. This gas helps the special helpers in our blood, called hemoglobin, to let go of the oxygen when it needs to be delivered to our cells and tissues. Scientists have found that when there's just the right amount of carbon dioxide (about 5%) in our blood, it is easiest for oxygen to reach our organs. CO2 is like a special helper that makes sure our body always gets the oxygen it needs to be healthy and strong. If there's too little carbon dioxide, it can make it hard for our body to get enough oxygen, and that can make us feel tired or sick. That's why it's important to make sure that we are not over-breathing and exhaling too much so that our body can always have the right amount of carbon dioxide to help us get the oxygen we need.

It's like a puzzle in which all the pieces need to fit together perfectly to work. Overall, the Bohr Effect is a special way that our body helps us to get the right amount of oxygen to all parts of it that need it, and it's important to keep the right amount of carbon dioxide in our blood to make sure that the oxygen gets to where it needs to go. There are some breathing conditions—like COPD and a few others—that cause a decrease in lung function, and so sufferers will build up excess CO2. If you have normal lung function, odds are you are more likely to be over-breathing because of how the respiratory system is designed.

2. "Just breathe more - the more air you put in your body the more oxygen gets into your muscles, heart and the rest of your body."

These half-truths are slowly killing us. When most people breathe more, they expel too much of their CO2, and as we just learned the body needs the right balance of CO2. So, as we breathe more and faster we are actually limiting our body's ability to transport oxygen to where it needs to go and exasperating the problem!

There is a medical term for this - hyperventilation. It can dramatically lower oxygen availability to your organs. You can have your (blood/oxygen) SPO2 meter that you put on your finger at 99% saturation, but if the partial pressure of CO2 in your body drops below 5% then the cascading effect is oxygen being tightly bound to the hemoglobin in your blood cells and so it will not be distributed optimally.

A few years ago, I had a friend who was convinced that if he just breathed more, he would be able to improve all aspects of his health. He was sure that the more air he put into his body, the more oxygen would get to his muscles and other organs. So one day, we decided to test this theory out by going on a hike. We hiked for 3 hours or so, with my friend taking deep breaths in an effort to get as much oxygen as possible into his body. I, on the other hand, practiced slow, deep breathing with controlled pauses on the inhale and exhale. At the end of our hike, I was ready for another 3 hours of hiking... and he looked exhausted and complained of a headache and nausea, to which someone joked, "Just breathe more!"

So, the idea that breathing more will help you calm down or get more oxygen to your organs is common but is not always valid. That is why people who hyperventilate for too long pass out. The body has to take over, because its oxygen levels have gotten too low. Although chronic hyperventilation has been shown to affect anxiety and stress levels, it has a negative cascading effect on the entire function of the body.

3. "It is hard to over breathe and I always need to breathe more air"

The mechanism of the respiratory system plays an important role in releasing excess CO2, as it is more common for humans to over breathe and expel too much of the gas. This system functions under the instruction of a center located within the brainstem, which acts as the 'boss' of breathing. Communications between this center and special receptors called chemoreceptors take place – these are like little detectives that monitor oxygen and CO2 levels in the blood.

When CO2 builds up beyond normal levels, these receptors alert the respiratory center and encourage deeper breathing in order to expel any extra CO2 and bring in fresh air for oxygenation. This system helps maintain healthy homeostasis by keeping oxygen and carbon dioxide levels balanced in our bodies.

4. "Lack of oxygen is what drives us to breathe"

Studies have shown that oxygen doesn't drive our respiratory system, CO2 build up does. Oxygen is important though, because it is needed for the body to function properly. However, it takes a long time for the body to adjust to different oxygen levels. For example, if someone moves to a higher altitude, it takes them a while to get used to the lower oxygen levels there (altitude sickness).

Under normal conditions, the body has enough oxygen, so changes in oxygen levels don't have a big impact on breathing.

However, when there is not enough oxygen, like during intense exercise or in an emergency, the body needs to breathe more to get more oxygen. The main way that breathing is controlled is through changes in the amount of carbon dioxide in the blood. This is because the body produces more carbon dioxide when it is using more energy, like when exercising. This extra carbon dioxide triggers the body to breathe more to get rid of it.

5. "I might breathe in too much CO2 and too much CO2 would make me sick or worse."

It is true that too much or too little CO2 has a negative effect on the body, and can even be fatal. Luckily, we live in a world where the air we breathe has 0.042% CO2 which is a very low level compared to what would make us sick. We also don't consume much CO2 from the atmosphere. Our bodies create the CO2 required for normal functioning as a byproduct of cellular activity, and our nervous systems are designed with an innate signal to prompt us to breathe when excessive amounts of this gas accumulate. It is unusual that oxygen levels provoke respiration; however, more research will reveal why these events occur so infrequently.

The debate over whether oxygen or carbon dioxide is more important for controlling breathing has been going on for a long time. Some scientists think oxygen is more important, while others think carbon dioxide is.

One group held that it is primarily the degree to which the blood is oxygenated that influences the respiratory center and controls its activity. The other presented evidence indicating that it is rather the amount of carbon dioxide in the blood that is the determining factor. Both sides of the controversy contributed experimental facts of value, and each was in part correct.

Respiration is, indeed, influenced fundamentally by the oxygen pressure to which the individual is acclimatized. This pressure depends upon elevation, as measured by the distance above sea level. But acclimatization to altitude is very slow, requiring days or weeks. It is only under conditions of sudden extreme oxygen deficiency, verging on asphyxia, or after intense muscular exertion, that respiration is stimulated.

Evidence to Settle the Debate:

The control of breathing and circulation has been studied extensively, with strong evidence suggesting that carbon dioxide plays a major role. This understanding began with research conducted by Haldane and Priestley, who published a paper called "The Regulation of Lung Ventilation." They were followed by other scientists, such as Douglas, who also contributed to the understanding of carbon dioxide's role in controlling respiration.

These studies have shown that changes in breathing are closely linked to the amount of carbon dioxide produced in the body, and that this is the main factor that controls breathing. Even slight changes in oxygen levels, such as those experienced at high altitudes, do not have a significant effect on breathing. Carbon dioxide is considered to be the main "respiratory hormone" in the body, controlling breathing and maintaining a constant level of carbon dioxide in the lungs. Carbon dioxide is the chief immediate respiratory hormone.

6. "You look stressed, take a deep breath"

While this is not exactly a misconception, most people don't understand what an optimal deep breath is and so their attempts to take one can have limited effects if they don't go deep, slow, and wide enough. For maximum benefit, the focus should be on diaphragm expansion. This is sometimes referred to as 'vertical breathing', or what I call 'big belly' or 'Buddha belly' breathing, or 'horizontal breathing' by some of my peers. The stomach muscle can expand across 360 degrees, not just forward. It's important to engage the entire stomach area—back, sides, and front—as this can create improved air movement and allow you to take bigger breaths. In fact, when done correctly, it allows you to create a vacuum in the lungs for deeper inhalation. It also gives you more time and control to take bigger breaths that are much deeper than upper chest breathing.

The additional benefits of focusing on big belly breathing is that you massage your digestive organs and lymph system (which is your body's waste removal system) gently. This is important, since the lymph system does not have any pumps and relies on bodily movements for circulation. Engaging in such breathing also increases gas exchange and minimizes any losses due to dead air space in the lungs.

This technique has to be mentioned here, while talking of stress, as the Buddha taught that the breath is a powerful tool for calming the mind and relieving stress. As Thich Nhat Hanh said, "Breathing in, I calm my body. Breathing out, I smile. Dwelling in the present moment I know this is a wonderful moment."

*7. "Weight loss and proper breathing have no effect on each
other"*

Weight loss and proper breathing are connected. Your breath can help you lose weight. We have to be balanced in our approach to everything in life, and when it comes to breathing this cannot be more true. We just talked about the importance of not breathing out too much CO2 and the benefits of it with the Bohr Effect. That being said, proper breathing will allow the right amount of CO2 to stay in your lungs and excess CO2 to leave, promoting optimal oxygen levels in your cells. When optimally oxygenated, these cells can function optimally. When we have breathing problems at night, our respiratory functioning is limited and therefore so is our disposal of CO2.

The presence of extra oxygen in the body while performing breathing exercises helps to burn the fat deposited in the body. This has been demonstrated in a great study which the news had a hard time understanding… but they did come up with a great headline! In December of 2014, an extraordinary study was published in the British Medical Journal that outlined exactly how much weight is lost simply through exhalation of CO2. Meerman and Brown ran the calculations and found that when 10 kg (around 22 pounds) of fat is fully broken down, in a process called oxidation, 18.5 pounds of it leaves the body as exhaled carbon dioxide and the rest is breathed out as water vapor.

"Our calculations show that the lungs are the primary excretory organ for fat," they wrote in their report. This actually explains why exercise helps people lose weight. The more breaths you take, the more CO2 you create and need to expel. And yes, you also lose weight just sitting on the couch watching TV and while you're asleep.

So, when it comes to weight loss, the key is breathing correctly and not holding your breath or over-breathing. There is no one answer to all problems, achieving the right balance is the best answer. The right balance varies according to what your body's unique needs are. If you're going to be putting your body under stress or working out intensely, you will need to breathe more.

Your cells will need more oxygen to remove excess CO_2. As you become more familiar with your role as breathing director, it will be easier for you to recognize and meet your body's needs in any given situation. Through practice and understanding, you can gain mastery of this skill!

8. "Too much CO2 will kill me"

At a high enough concentration level, yes. But there seems to be an optimal level for breathing function and an optimal level for a short period of time when the body is in need of repair. I will give examples of healthy and lethal amounts of CO_2.

I remember when I first heard this and was shocked. It was at the 29th birthday party of a popular blogger in Russia. The party had 55 lbs of dry ice (frozen CO_2) thrown into a pool, which people jumped into. The vast amount of CO_2 released was enough to kill 3 people and hospitalize 7 others. This sad event is a reminder that exposure to a substance beyond a healthy range can prove deadly. This next section will show the healthy range of CO_2 and its possible benefits.

CO2 Levels Research

The power of CO_2 in different proportions has been studied by many researchers, but most interesting to me is that conducted by Yandel Henderson. Pneumonia, post-surgery anesthesia, and asphyxia were just a few of the variables in his trials. Much of his work is in current use or still being studied to this day to determine the effectiveness of short term CO_2 for health benefits. Let's take a deeper dive into his work.

Baseline Breathing

In Anesthesia

In 1920, Henderson, Haggard, and Coburn took their research into a clinical setting. They observed that when patients were given inhalations of carbon dioxide (8%) after major surgical operations and under open ether anesthesia, the results were positive. The patients' deep breathing returned, cyanosis disappeared, their skin changed from blue-gray and cold to pink and warm, their pulse improved, and arterial pressure returned to normal.

Additionally, the anesthetic was rapidly eliminated from the blood, consciousness returned quickly, and nausea and vomiting were reduced or eliminated. They also found that when slow hemorrhage occurred after operations on the brain, the rate of breathing gradually decreased, but in several cases, lives were saved by stimulating respiration with inhalations of carbon dioxide.

In continuation of these observations, it was also found that when slow hemorrhage occurs after operations upon the brain, the rate of breathing gradually decreases until death is imminent. In several such cases, lives were saved by stimulation of respiration with inhalations of carbon dioxide.

Prevalence of carbon dioxide inhalation is now common in connection with anesthesia, and nearly every American anesthetic apparatus has an attachment for a cylinder of carbon dioxide or a mixture of carbon dioxide and oxygen. This approach really is that effective at counteracting respiratory depression during the operation and at stimulating respiration and inducing rapid elimination of anesthetic afterwards. It also helps to restore vigorous heart action and the tonus of the peripheral circulation.

Pneumonia

The use of carbon dioxide inhalation therapy as a potential treatment for medical pneumonia, specifically after influenza, has been tested in the past and is currently under active investigation. Studies by Henderson, Haggard, Coryllos, and Birnbaum have revealed that in dogs with experimentally induced pneumonia, the lungs can be cleared and pneumonia cured by placing the animals in an atmosphere of about 8% carbon dioxide for 12 to 24 hours.

This is because the growth of pneumococci, the bacteria that causes pneumonia, is inhibited and they can even be killed by a lowering of pH to levels no greater than carbon dioxide may induce. Furthermore, many cases of pneumonia have been treated with inhalations of carbon dioxide in oxygen, and a special tent for this treatment was introduced by Henderson and Haggard. Those who have used it believe that this treatment is superior to oxygen alone. The use of carbon dioxide inhalation therapy is promising as a non-invasive and efficient treatment for pneumonia.

Asphyxia of the Newborn

The use of inhalation treatment to treat asphyxia in newborns has evolved out of the treatment of carbon monoxide poisoning. Rescue crews of the Chicago Fire Department played a crucial role in this development. Many times, doctors were unable to induce active, natural breathing in newborns using traditional methods such as swinging, spanking, and dipping the child in cold and hot water. In these cases, they would call the rescue crews and use their inhalators to provide assistance. This proved so successful that within a couple of years, the fire department had developed a considerable practice in this field. With justifiable pride, it claimed the saving of several hundred babies.

Baseline Breathing

In theory and in application, inhalation of oxygen and carbon dioxide is the most effective method for combating asphyxia in newborns. This realization led to chemical stimulation and support for the depressed respiratory center of newborn children by inhalation of carbon dioxide rapidly replacing the older, and often ineffective, methods of resuscitation depending upon cutaneous stimulation. However, this treatment should only be administered under the guidance and supervision of a qualified medical professional.

Carbogen is the name this mixture is most commonly called. The ratio of CO_2 to oxygen can range, but 5% CO_2 and 95% O_2 seems to be the most studied. In the last 20 years, there has been a resurgence of CO_2 and oxygen studies for different health issues. Carbogen is used for carbon monoxide poisoning and has found its way into many fire departments' tool kits. Canada has been using it in treatments for COPD. China and Japan in the last 10 years have been using it to improve athletic performance.

It is clear that carbon dioxide has a wide range of uses and benefits, from aiding in anesthesia to treating pneumonia. While too much CO_2 can be dangerous, there are also optimal levels for short-term use which have been studied by many researchers. Breathing correctly, with the right balance of oxygen and CO_2, can help you lose weight, improve your athletic performance, and even save lives in cases of carbon monoxide poisoning or newborn asphyxia. The power of proper breathing should not be underestimated - it can provide great health benefits when done properly!

Chapter 4
Breathwork Mechanics

Breathwork is like the engine of your body: it can power you through physical activity, give life to your mental clarity, and be the source of your strength. No wonder then, that for centuries various cultures have used breathwork as a means to promote health and well-being. Just as the right fuel can power an engine, breathing correctly can have a profound effect on your whole body, both physically and mentally.

In this chapter, we take a deep dive into the biomechanics of breathing. By that I mean the anatomy involved in taking our next breath and how different types of breathwork can truly make a difference.

Nasal Breathing Versus Mouth Breathing

Whenever I used to get overwhelmed by what life was throwing at me, my grandma would always tell me, "Take a deep breath in through your nose." It seemed counterintuitive at the time... wasn't breathing through my mouth easier? But, as it turns out, nasal breathing is incredibly important and effective.

If you remember one thing from this chapter, let it be this perfect phrase, "Follow your nose." Your nose leads your body in many ways. It is physically the organ that leads the body anatomically and with breathing, it conditions the air for optimal gas exchange in the lungs, it filters our particles, and humidifies and pressurizes the air before being introduced to the lungs. Nasal passages also create nitric oxide that is toxic to viruses.

Your nose is for breathing and your mouth is for eating, it is that simple. It is a heavy truth once you understand the science and the effect of using the nose for primary breathing. Nasal breathing conditions your breathing pattern toward diaphragmatic, slow breathing and away from shallow, fast chest breathing.

Dr. Maurice Cottle in 1954 stated that the nose performs over 30 functions which have important roles and are related to the heart, lungs, and the body as a whole. The nose is directly connected to the primary breathing muscle, the diaphragm. Meanwhile, the mouth is linked directly to the upper chest. Breathing quickly through the mouth, relying on the upper chest, is a method of breathing that is simply not efficient and which also decreases the amount of oxygen reaching the lungs.

Science Behind the Benefits of Nasal Breathing

The nose is designed to prepare air for the lungs and gas exchange. It filters the air, warms, humidifies, sterilizes, and maintains the proper pressure in the lungs for optimal gas exchange. Nasal breathing offers an increase of 10-20% more oxygen uptake, it removes large amounts of germs and bacteria from the air and keeps them away from the lungs, and during physical exercise it can help increase HRV and VO2 max.

Taking in air through the nose has been proven to provide up to 16 times more nitric oxide than breathing with your mouth! This added nitric oxide helps promote better gas exchange in our lungs and can even assist the immune system by killing off harmful viruses and bacteria! Aside from that, nasal breathing also comes with a plethora of other benefits such as boosting one's circulation, pain relief, emotional well-being, and sexual health.

There is never a bad age to start breathing through the nose, but the sooner the better. But you're not really starting from scratch. As I mentioned, nasal breathing is normally the way babies and toddlers breathe from birth. Over time, they pick up bad habits and transition to more mouth breathing. As adults, the best way to restart nasal breathing is with a few simple exercises and habits.

My Take on Mouth Breathing

Mouth breathing at certain times is understandable and appropriate, but too much can be detrimental to overall health. Chronic mouth breathing can be a source of high stress levels, as it sends a signal to our bodies that we are in fight-or-flight mode. This constant state of alertness weakens the immune system and increases feelings of anxiety... something no one wants! By switching from mouth breathing to nasal inhalation, you may see an improvement in your mental health and physical well being fairly quickly.

If you or your child are habitual mouth breathers, it's important to understand the risks. Research has found that mouth breathing can lead to a number of issues such as increased dehydration, acidification of the mouth, cavities, gum disease, bad breath, snoring, and sleep apnea. It can also contribute to poor posture and decreased respiratory health. So be mindful while monitoring your or your child's breathing, and work on improving those habits to stay healthy, safe, and optimally functional.

Mouth breathing was one of the biggest personal breathing problems and breakthroughs I had. I did many things to adjust to nasal breathing, and it took some discipline.

The first thing I did was use mouth tape. Sounds scary, I know, so I started slowly by using it for just a few hours during the day. I was still nervous about trying the tape at night, but I'd heard such great feedback from others that I eventually tried it. It was much easier than I thought! Weird? Yes, but the impact was wild. I woke up feeling more energetic, no middle of the night wake up, no dry mouth in the morning, and every night after it got easier.

It may sound odd to use tape on your child's mouth, but trust me it is far less disturbing than it sounds. Kids can use a mouth tape called *Myo Tape* which doesn't actually cover the mouth, so they can still breathe through their mouth if they need to. It is applied around the mouth, with only some light tension, and works as a reminder to use their nose. I also prefer to train with mouth tape during the day for a while. When they are watching a show or a movie is a great time to use the Myo Tape to have them gain awareness of and focus on breathing through their nose. The nice thing about kids is that they seem to adapt much faster than adults. I have seen kids' habits change within a few weeks, and stay with them for years.

My neighbors' son had a habit of mouth breathing. No matter how many times his parents tried to get him to switch to nasal breathing, he would always go back to mouth breathing. That is until one day, when his parents decided to take drastic measures. They taped his mouth during the day so he couldn't mouth breathe! It was a last-ditch effort that worked! Without being able to breathe through his mouth, their son started nasal breathing properly and soon the habit stuck. While it may sound extreme, this trick works surprisingly well... just remember not to leave the tape on for too long!

Another tip for an optimal mouth-taping experience is that a little chapstick should be applied to the lips prior to laying down the tape. This will ensure that the adhesive won't take a layer of skin off your lips when removed.

I do like to let the kids know there are many benefits to nasal breathing, and giving them reasons to stick with it like this has proven very effective. I will tell them how nasal breathing increases your intelligence and sports performance, and can help them get better sleep. Then I will also explain the problems with mouth breathing such as crooked teeth, bad breath, and cavities.

Importance of Posture

You're probably no stranger to working on a computer and the irritating neck and back pain that creeps up as a result. Gotta love bad posture! And you aren't alone, lots of people have this problem. In fact, a study showed that people's tweets about back pain increased by 84% in 2020 compared to the year before. Poor posture can be a major contributor to the discomfort we experience. Did you know that poor posture isn't just bad for our backs and necks, but that it can also be detrimental to our breathing?

Dr. Belisa Vranich—clinical psychologist and author of the book "Breathe"—knows a thing or two about how optimal breathing is linked to good posture. It all comes back to the fact that, when you slouch, your chest collapses inward and forces your diaphragm down, making it harder for your lungs to take in air. Compare that to sitting up straight or standing tall, which opens up your chest and allows for easier inhalation and exhalation of air that results in a boost of energy and focus.

If you have good posture (keeping your spine straight and your head up) you can help avoid back pain and breathe better. But there's more to it than just avoiding back pain. Spinal experts say that there are lots of benefits to be enjoyed from sitting up straight. Some of them are listed below:

1. Optimizes circulation

Optimizing circulation is crucial when it comes to ensuring that your body receives the necessary oxygen and nutrients to perform optimally. Good posture can aid in this process by facilitating easy circulation to all your bodily tissues and organs, allowing for efficient delivery of essential nutrients. Conversely, poor posture can hinder circulation and compromise your overall efficacy.

A good analogy to describe the importance of good posture in promoting circulation is that of a hose. Just as a kink in a hose can obstruct the flow of water, poor posture can obstruct the flow of blood and other essential nutrients in your body. However, correcting your posture can alleviate these obstructions, enabling unhindered circulation.

2. Increases lung capacity and function

Think of your lungs like the hose from the analogy again. When you slouch, there's limited space for your lungs to expand and fill with air. However, good posture provides ample space for your lungs to function properly and take in as much air as needed. Additionally, good posture creates a conducive environment for deep breathing, which can aid in relaxation and respiration.

3. Improves energy levels and improves organ functioning

Good posture supports good communication between your brain and your organs through your nervous system. This is because your nerves travel from your brain and down your spinal cord to your organs. Straight routes are more direct, so having a straight spine helps ensure rapid communication. Therefore, good posture leads to better functioning of your organs, while poor posture can negatively impact communication and reduce performance. Regular exercise, which helps maintain good posture, will also benefit the health of your organs.

Breathing Cadence/Rate

Cadence breathing is a form of rhythmic breathing that can help shift the autonomic system. Breathing cadence is an important tool to help you maximize your breathing and get the most out of every breath. By inhaling and exhaling at a steady, equal tempo, you can increase the amount of oxygen that enters your lungs with each breath. This can help boost your aerobic and cardiovascular endurance, as well as provide general calming benefits. You can practice breathing cadence by counting to three each time you inhale or exhale in order to maintain a consistent rhythm.

Some benefits of cadence breathing include:

- Calming the mind and body
- Improving breath control
- Increasing oxygen uptake
- Enhancing blood circulation
- Improving heart function
- Increasing blood flow to the brain
- Boosting overall body coherence

Researchers Dr. Patricia Gerbarg and Dr. Richard Brown use cadence breathing to work with patients with anxiety and depression. They tried the idea of slowing the breathing rate to 5.5 breaths a minute. Most of the group found themselves in a better mental space/mood as a result. They did find that it was hard for a few to feel comfortable with the 5-second inhales, so they tried beginning with a 3-second breath rate until they were comfortable and then slowly progressing to the 5-second rate.

Gerbarg and Brown wrote books and published articles about the benefits of slow breathing, and this technique became known as 'resonant breathing'. The best part of cadence breathing is that it can be done anywhere and at any time, without anyone even noticing you're doing it. I like to tell people this is as close as you can get to meditating by just breathing that you can get.

You might not be surprised that the breathing pattern while saying a Catholic Rosary has the same breathing pattern of 5.5 breaths a minute. This was also found to be the case with many Buddhist mantras, Native American prayers, and other religions' prayers. They all create an experience that mimics the 5.5 breaths/minute pattern. This particular cadence has many positive effects on the body. When they say prayer is powerful and can heal, there might be real science behind that! And you don't have to be religious to get the benefit of prayer, just apply the 5.5 breathing rate. The changes in physiology are consistent and observable.

When you break the pattern, and start talking or return to your normal breathing, the benefits and peak body coherence dissipate.

Breathing Volume

The total volume of air you breathe into your lungs a minute is known as tidal volume. This can vary from person to person depending on their size, age, and the activity they are engaged in. Generally speaking, the average adult has a tidal volume of around 500 ml per breath, while children have anywhere between 200-400ml. This is a very interesting subject because of the patterns that show up with health issues and breathing volume.

Baseline Breathing

I must reiterate here that correlation doesn't equal causation... but I believe it is still worth looking at. The connection between breathing and diseases has been the subject of numerous studies, leading some to question whether there is a cause-and-effect relationship in some cases. Over-breathing, or hyperventilation, has been linked to a decrease in oxygen circulation throughout the body and reduced cell function. This can result in immediate symptoms such as dizziness, fatigue, headaches, chest pain, and lightheadedness. All of these can diminish one's quality of life and lead to further health concerns if not addressed. Understanding how our breath affects our physical health is an important part of developing an overall wellness strategy that encourages proper breathing habits.

This subject was well studied by a Russian, Dr. Buteyko, who created the 'Buteyko Method' and suggested that "Breathing Slower and Less is The Greatest Health Discovery Ever". One of his students, Dr. Artour Rakhimov, continued his work and put together breathing pattern studies related to illness. The patterns that emerged are very interesting.

The breathing volume for a healthy human is around 6-7L of air per minute.
Heart Disease studies range from 12-16L/minute
Diabetes: 10-15L air per minute
Cystic fibrosis: 10-18L/minute
Panic disorder: 12L/minute
Bipolar Disorder: 11L/minute

I have another theory that is anecdotal, but which I believe merits further research - breathing volumes may have increased over the last 100 years or more.

A number of studies have observed a rise in average breathing volume since the 1920s and 1930s, with an average range between 4.6L and 5.5L per minute. This trend has seemingly been consistent since the 1950s. It is unclear what may be causing people to breathe more air by volume per minute, but it appears that this uptick has been shown in a handful of studies. It seems to have been increasing since WWII by unhealthy volume/minute levels.

Breathing volume studies over the last 60- 70 years. We know that over-breathing has detrimental effects on our health, so why the increase?

Shock	1939	average 5.5L/M	age 27-43	46 male subjects
Shock	1939	average 4.6L/M	age 27-42	40 female subjects
Matheson	1950	average 6.9L/M		100 subjects
DeLorey	1999	average 10L/M	age 35-43	20 subjects
Narliewicz	2006	average 8.5L/M	age 22-40	69 subjects
Traver	2008	average 12L/M	age 60-64	20 subjects

Emotional and Mental Performance

It cannot be emphasized enough how powerful a tool breathwork is for enhancing emotional and mental performance. It involves using conscious breathing techniques to explore, regulate, and stimulate the mind-body connection. Breathwork provides many tangible benefits including improved focus, greater clarity of thought, deeper relaxation, and stress relief. Let's explore the depths of these powerful links:

The Power of the Vagus Nerve

When we breathe, we either stimulate or inhibit our vagus nerve. Every day, most of us are unconsciously inhibiting and stimulating our vagus nerve without even realizing it. The vagus nerve is a complex of nerve pathways that run our nervous system, with breathing being one of its biggest modulators.

Baseline Breathing

When we deeply exhale, we tell the vagus nerve to send a relaxation signal to the rest of the body. When we inhale, it has the opposite effect on the vagus nerve. Studies suggest that the vagus nerve influences inflammation, blood pressure, mood, and heart rate.

Technically, we call the two modes of the autonomic nervous system sympathetic and parasympathetic—fight or flight mode and rest and digest—and studies have shown that slow diaphragmatic breathing can stimulate the vagus nerve and trigger our parasympathetic response. Likewise, when we breathe fast and shallow, it can trigger a sympathetic response. Breathing and the vagus nerve never shut off and are always in flux and responding to each other. With this understanding, we can see how powerful changes of breathing patterns can be for the entire body, especially the nervous system.

After reading about the glorious power of the vagus nerve and how breathing exercises can help activate it, let's take part in a brief exercise. We'll begin by taking three deep breaths through our noses while focusing on bringing air into our diaphragms, then slowly exhale out through the nose for at least 6 seconds. Ensure that your exhalation is longer than your inhalation - this should be done for a period of 2 minutes.

The effect you should be feeling is a result of the increased level of oxygen made available to your brain. It should reduce stress and increase functioning, which will help your brain find solutions and resolve problems easier. The upset feeling should start to settle. This exercise of slow exhalation is a great way to remain calm and stay cool.

Physical Performance

But how can I apply these breathing ideas in my physical exercise and performance? Good question. Baseline Breathing protocols are what I have people focus on in their pursuit of optimal breathing for physical performance, from professional athletes to seniors going on daily walks.

By the way, daily walks are my favorite physical exercise that I use to condition myself for changing breathing behavior. It is a slow-paced exercise, yes, but it starts to build muscle memory and optimal breathing habits for your body in a low stress environment. It makes the transition to heavy weights or high-intensity cardio with functional breathing a bit more habitual. This breathing practice will, over time, also improve your body's CO_2 tolerance.

One of the main principles of applying Baseline Breathing rules is to pace your breathing to keep good form. This is not as easy as it sounds, and may take much more mental effort than physical to maintain good form in your breath movement, only nasal breathing, and mindful breath cadence. It takes time to build up your breathing strength, and should be done with conscious intention. Once you can comfortably do the Baseline Breathing protocols for an entire exercise session it's okay to start pushing yourself further.

Slower Cadence Breathing

By not over-breathing you allow your body to keep proper CO_2 levels in the lungs. This facilitates optimal oxygen absorption and distribution throughout the body. It might create a slight feeling of air hunger or some minor discomfort, but should be nothing more. If you do feel anything more than slight discomfort, change the pace of your physical exercise to match your breathing rate or take a break until you can control your breathing. So, in short, 5 breaths per minute is the goal.

Baseline Breathing

Deep Belly Breathing

This is something that, over time, you can condition your body to concentrate on. Deep belly breathing (or Buddha belly style breathing) involves diaphragmatic muscles so the lungs can expand more, increasing oxygen uptake and creating an increased vacuum effect. You are looking to have the most effective breathing while doing physical exercise, but it is common to fall into old breathing habits. We just need to adjust as we become aware of slipping back like this.

The first few weeks are the most challenging because of how much mental focus is needed, both on the placement and pace of the breath. As your body gets used to the changes, you'll slowly find these adjustments becoming almost instinctive. The effects of better HRV, increasing your VO2 max, and increasing your endurance potential are all parts of the reward. So, you may understandably be excited about the changes that will start to take place in the first month in your overall cardio health and performance!

Ultimately, by engaging with breathwork we learn to step out of reactive patterns in our lives and move towards living in more conscious awareness. When used correctly, it can have profound effects on both emotional and mental performance, as well as enhance our capacity for physical exercise and athletic performance. Through understanding the biomechanics of breathwork, and learning various breathing techniques, we can start to unlock the potential within ourselves to achieve greater balance and wellbeing. So, bring the techniques mentioned above into practice today!

Chapter 5
Baseline Breathing Protocol

Breathing keeps us alive and grounded. Much like a clock, regular deep breaths help to set our internal rhythm and keep us in time with ourselves. In the same way that we adjust an alarm clock to time our wake-up call, adjusting our breathing using a Baseline Breathing protocol helps to reset our natural rhythm and restore balance in both mind and body. Through this chapter, we will explore how to practice Baseline Breathing correctly in order to maximize these positive effects.

What makes Baseline Breathing different from any other breathing practice is our protocols. We educate, practice, and apply on a foundational level for long-term breathing adjustments.

There are many different styles and advanced forms of breathwork. I have tried nearly every one that I could find. I have trained others in a variety of breathwork techniques and, after a lot of feedback and testing, have found these core principles. They are what created Baseline Breathing. Baseline Breathing is a term used to refer to an individual's natural breathing rate or pattern. It can be thought of as the foundation upon which all other breathwork, relaxation, and meditation practices are built and it is essential in understanding how we interact with our environment and when it comes to tracking our progress over time.

We must understand the physical and chemical mechanics of breathing. With this knowledge, we can get more out of our breathing exercises and conditioning. When you are able to apply more breathing control—and do so with an understanding of why it works—you will find more real-life applications becoming second nature. When we truly comprehend the power of breath, exercise and practice come into play in order to enhance our functioning. However, it's only when these two are combined that incredible growth can take place. Therefore, we practice proper breathing exercises while staying aware of the feedback that our body is giving us. This breathwork foundation is to create an unbreakable breath. This is your baseline. From that solid footing you can go on to pursue all your physical and mental endeavors in life.

BBP was designed for everyone, from our kids to our grandparents, and was created to help you adjust your habits without ever expending too much energy. This can be the starting point for even more advanced breathwork training and from which you can grow your new habits of functional breathing. By having less dysfunctional breathing, you can have more control and awareness of your breath and get the most out of your everyday life.

Baseline Breathing Rules

There are a few key rules to follow when engaging in Baseline Breathing. These simple steps will help you develop deep breathing habits and reap the maximum benefits of this practice.

1. We primarily focus on doing breathwork with the mouth closed. The respiratory system works best with clean,

humidified, warm, and partially pressurized air. Therefore, we emphasize breathing through the nose, for both inhaling and exhaling. While there will be plenty of times when this will not work, if ever given the choice, the nose is where the breath should flow through. If you have nasal polyps or a deviated septum like me, it may take a little more time to get used to it. We train to step down with nasal only breathing only under strain, then we adapt by inhaling through the nose and exhaling through the mouth. The last mode is mouth only breathing, and there are certainly times when this is optimal… though these are only short periods of time. For example, if you are swimming laps or are in high-energy training, some form of mouth breathing might be best. But for the other 99% of the occasions, we follow the nose!

2. Breathe with a deep, big belly breath. This deep, wide, belly breath is the ideal breath. So, practice expanding your stomach from all sides like a balloon. Placing the air in the lower lungs is how you get the best gas exchange in the lungs. There is about 150ml of dead space in your lungs that isn't used for gas exchange. So, when we breathe deeper we give our lungs more air to exchange with. There is naturally more blood flow in the bottom of the lungs, so lower is where you want the air to go. In addition to this, by breathing with the diaphragm you are massaging digestive organs and helping your lymph system detox your body.

3. Keep your breath controlled, slow, and rhythmic. Over time, your body will start to adapt and this will become more automatic with practice. The first 2 rules give you the highest quality air and at the right quantity for your lungs. We have no need to breathe fast or hyperventilate. With slow breathing, we can keep the optimal CO_2 partial pressure in the lungs, and so we can get optimal oxygen absorption throughout the body. Creating the most energy-efficient respiratory system we can is our goal. We have a good reference of 5.5 breaths a minute, that

can be adjusted to our body's needs, but 5.5 breaths a minute is a great baseline.

CO2 Tolerance

Now that you are familiar with the basics of baseline breathing, it's time to explore how to incorporate this exercise into your daily life. In addition, in order to begin, a question arises - what is your current CO2 tolerance level and breathing mode? To find out for yourself, let's explore different breather groups.

Survival breathing - that is what we call the unconscious, automatic type of breathing that is characterized by mouth-breathing that is shallow, happens in the upper chest, features poor mechanics, has low-stress control and a high sensitivity to carbon dioxide. This style of breathing is associated with a Bolt score of 10-20 or less, and a CO2 tolerance test result of 20 or less. Survival breathing can lead to hyperventilation and over-breathing, both of which can have negative impacts on overall health if left untreated or unmanaged.

Functional breathing is a breath practice focused on developing more control over both breathing rate and cadence. It involves limited over-breathing, good breathing mechanics, and above average stress control. This type of breathing typically results in a Bolt score of 20-30, and a CO2 tolerance test result of between 20 and 40. Through regular practice, functional breathing can lead to improved physiological health.

Finally, comes thriving/optimal/high-performance breathing. This is the highest level of breath practice, and results in superior control over the autonomic nervous system. It involves increased CO2 tolerance, great breathing mechanics, good stress control, and a very high Bolt Score (above 30). A high CO2 Tolerance test result (40 and above) indicates excellent pulmonary health.

Why does CO2 tolerance matter?

CO2 tolerance refers to the amount of carbon dioxide that your body can tolerate before triggering a response. By increasing your CO2 tolerance, you train your body to handle temporary imbalances better and slow down your breathing cadence. This can improve your body's ability to adapt to stressors.

One expert on CO2 tolerance and breathwork is Patrick McKeown, and he is also a leading authority on the Buteyko Breathing Method. He has written extensively on the subject, including the book "The Oxygen Advantage: The Simple, Scientifically Proven Breathing Techniques for a Healthier, Slimmer, Faster, and Fitter You," which includes information on CO2 tolerance and its role in optimizing breathing for better health and performance. In the book, McKeown explains how practicing breath-holding exercises and gradually increasing CO2 tolerance can improve lung function, increase oxygen delivery to the body's tissues, and improve athletic performance.

The benefits of improving CO2 tolerance are short term and long-term. When you engage in activities such as endurance training, CO2 builds up in the body, causing your blood to become acidic. This triggers the need to exhale in order to get rid of that CO2. Improving your CO2 tolerance works in a similar way to building strength in your muscles... and it also takes time and practice.

High CO2 tolerance can also boost your aerobic metabolism. According to the Bohr Effect, when blood CO2 levels are high and blood pH is low, it's easier for your body to absorb oxygen. Increasing CO2 tolerance can improve oxygen delivery to cells.

A poor CO2 tolerance indicates poor breathing control, which makes it harder to absorb oxygen under stress. To improve your body's overall ability to handle stressors, you need strong breathing muscles and excellent breathing control. This way, your lungs and respiratory system can handle stress efficiently and lead the way.

As your CO2 tolerance improves, your body can handle higher levels of CO2 before entering emergency mode, where it triggers hyperventilation and an intense need to exhale and regulate your breath. For athletes, this can mean improved endurance and the ability to push themselves further. For everyone else, this can mean better regulated emotions and increased mental abilities.

There's a strong connection between CO2 tolerance and stress/anxiety. The better control you have over your breathing, the less anxiety you'll experience. You'll also be better equipped to handle stressful environments or situations.

So, whether you're an athlete or an office worker, managing anxiety and arousal through your nervous system is essential for health and performance. Low anxiety leads to low cortisol, which in turn leads to less fat, more muscle, and improved physical and mental well being.

How to Calculate CO2 Tolerance:

The first step to tracking your progress is to measure your current CO2 tolerance level. The CO2 tolerance test is a simple and effective tool to assess your body's response to stress. According to experts, understanding your body's response to stress is the key to finding your CO2 tolerance.

This can be done either with a device such as the Respirometer, or by taking a simple test at home. By using only a stopwatch, you can get a glimpse into the state of your body's CO2 tolerance levels.

This test was first used by rescue divers to train themselves to hold their breath for longer periods. It has since been researched and developed by performance training expert Andrew Huberman at Stanford University.

The CO2 tolerance test measures your body's ability to adapt to new situations without becoming overly stressed. A well-adapted body is a sign of good health and a key predictor of happiness.

Here's how to perform the CO2 tolerance test:

1. Get your stopwatch ready.
2. Take three breaths in and out through your nose.
3. Take one more breath, filling your lungs all the way up.
4. Start the stopwatch as you begin to exhale this breath.
5. Let the breath out as slowly as possible, trying to extend it.
6. If you hold your breath or swallow, start over.
7. Stop the timer when you run out of air.

Your CO2 tolerance test results can provide insight into your body's stress levels:

- < 20 seconds: Your CO2 tolerance needs improvement.
- 20-40 seconds: Average results for most people.
- 40-60 seconds: Above average, representing good CO2 tolerance.
- 60 seconds: Indicates a healthy pulmonary system and good stress and breath control.

Bolt Score

The next factor to consider is your Bolt score. This score is not a measurement of how long you can hold your breath, but an assessment of your breathing profile that reflects how well your body responds to stress and how effectively you can move through breath cycles.

It is important for individuals with asthma, anxiety, and panic disorder as it can reflect their breathing patterns. However, even those who are elite athletes often start with low BOLT scores.

The BOLT score is affected by several factors, including sensitivity to carbon dioxide (CO2), airway constriction, discomfort in the diaphragm, and psychological factors such as anxiety or fear of suffocation. With daily practice of breathing exercises, BOLT scores can be improved.

Your BOLT score is also related to your breathlessness during physical activities. If your score is low, it can be improved with breathing exercises. The BOLT score ranges from below 10 seconds (which is characterized by noisy, irregular, and labored breathing), to 40 seconds (which is considered normal for individuals who exercise regularly).

A BOLT score of 10-20 seconds can be improved with breathing exercises to reduce breathlessness, improve sleep quality, and enhance overall health and fitness. A score of 20-30 seconds is considered good, but there are still benefits to improving it further.

Practicing breathing exercises can help increase your BOLT score by reducing sensitivity to CO2 and resetting the breathing center in the brain. The goal is to increase the BOLT score to 40 seconds, which can be achieved with dedication and practice.

Improving the BOLT score is also key to increasing physical endurance. When tolerance to carbon dioxide improves, individuals can achieve a higher VO2 max and enhance their performance. The "Oxygen Advantage" program aims to help increase your BOLT score to maximize your potential.

However, keep in mind that your bolt score is only for adults and has no reliability for children.

How to Calculate Bolt Score:

Before measuring your BOLT score, it's important to rest for 10 minutes. Make sure to read the instructions carefully and have a timer ready. Ideally, the test should be taken first thing in the morning, but you can take it anytime you're ready.

Here's how to take the test:

1. Take a normal breath in through your nose, and then breathe out through your nose.
2. Cover your nose with your fingers to prevent air from entering your lungs.
3. Start the timer.
4. Time how many seconds it takes for you to feel the urge to breathe, or the first signs of your body telling you to breathe. This could be the need to swallow, constricted airways, or involuntary contractions of your breathing muscles. Note that the BOLT score measures how quickly your body reacts to a lack of air, *not* how long you can hold your breath.
5. When you feel the urge to breathe, release your nose and stop the timer.
6. Take a calm breath through your nose.
7. Resume normal breathing.

This looks like it has nothing to do with practical life, right? Recently, I helped my friend think otherwise. That friend was having a panic attack, and I encouraged her to try some breathwork to help calm herself down. She did what we call "box breathing" (inhaling for four counts, holding for four counts, exhaling for four counts, and holding for four counts).

We also tested her Bolt Score to change her mental focus onto breathing. After about ten minutes of this practice, she felt much calmer and in control of the situation. It was amazing to see how this simple exercise can have such an immediate calming effect on the nervous system. Speaking of which, I'm reminded here of an out of this world meditation technique, the application of which follows all Baseline Breathing protocols.

5 Second Buddha Meditation

I have been in many meditation classes, and worked with a few daily meditations, but have never found a practice that was satisfactory. There was always an uncomfortable friction that hindered me from reaching the results I was looking for.

I remember working with a group on cadence breathing, and during the class feeling meditative-like peace. The group agreed with me and asked if they wanted to try to make this even more peaceful. The group was on board with it, so I asked everyone to close their eyes, use the 5 and 5 cadence breathing, place some attention on just the count and let any thoughts that showed up drift away. If thoughts persisted, I instructed them to focus back on the 5-second count and use their diaphragm completely.

The feedback was amazing that day. I was surprised by the mental states that we all were getting to in less than 10 minutes. So, I asked everyone to try this at home and give me some more feedback. I then started to use it myself, and found it progressively easier to start and stay in it as long as I liked, with very little resistance. I tried doing a 1-minute version of this meditation in the middle of the day and was blown away by the level of mental peace and calm I could accumulate.

I didn't hear that much from the group until nearly a month later. Every single person had nearly the same response - they couldn't believe how easy this was, and they wanted to see if over the month the effects changed. Most of them weren't seasoned meditators or yogis, they were simply striving to become healthier through breathwork. The tool I created is one of my greatest gifts that I can share with others, and I hope you do too!

For the people that can't meditate, or find it uncomfortable, this can be your go-to breathing exercise. This meditation can be practiced by anyone, regardless of their religious or spiritual beliefs. You can start implementing with very little time.

It is simple, but highly effective.

5 Second Buddha Meditation Method

Well, the guidelines to follow are straightforward.

> 1st: As you count, restrict yourself to 5 second breaths - both inhaling and exhaling.
> 2nd: Focus on your breathing form - belly breathing and inhaling and exhaling exclusively through your nose.

That is it! When a thought pops into your mind, don't judge it or get frustrated that it's there. Instead, gently focus back on the 5-second breath count. You don't need to force the thought out, and sometimes it is even okay to let the thought be completed and then continue.

If you feel your shoulder start to lift or you feel yourself shallow chest breathing, bring your breath back to your diaphragm. Thoughts will jump in. Like I said, sometimes you can let them play out! But remember to have your focus return to the breath count and your belly afterwards.

For the first 30 days, I would typically start off with 5 to 10 minutes. Over time, 30 minutes or more became very easy and comfortable. After 30 days of finding such a quick and easy meditation state, I felt almost an addiction to the state of peace it brought. I then found myself easily going much past the 30 minute mark.

One of the best parts of this breathing meditation pattern is that you can do it almost anywhere, with eyes closed or open! Of course, it is easier with your eyes closed, but the feedback from others is mixed. So feel free to find the style that works best for you.

I practice when I wake up and before I get ready to sleep. I also can use it during the day to make little mental shifts. I have been practicing for a long time, so as soon as I start to count to 5 on my breath, my mental state will start to shift. My mental focus goes to the 5-second breath count and my breathing goes deep into my diaphragm. Those two thoughts seem to keep my brain busy enough to disengage and shift to better body-mind cohesion. You may notice that your body takes a few minutes to respond in the beginning, but after a few months it can become nearly instant.

So for a 5-second meditation, remember to shift your awareness to where your breath is going in your body (diaphragm/belly) and start that count of 5 seconds for either exhale or inhale. You may not need to keep the 5-second count going, and can find your own pace that works, though I would use the 5-second count initially to maintain a strong foundation whenever your thoughts wander. And your thoughts may wonder! Use the count as your focus to recenter. Some people get upset or frustrated when they can't stop their thoughts, and I ask them to change their perspective. That shift changes everything. You are not trying to stop your mind, just observe your thoughts as if they were logs on a river. You ground your mind by returning it to your breath count. It is simple, but not always easy. With practice, you get better and quicker.

Baseline Breathing

Feedback has shown me that it works faster and becomes easier the more you do it, but even without practice the shift is noticeable within a few minutes. So, the next time you need some creativity, stress management, or just a few minutes of peace, try the 5-second meditation. Play around with the count in reverse, going from 5 to 1.

There is one other breathing meditation that I would like to talk about. It has many of the same guidelines as the 5-second meditation but is made for relaxing your autonomic system. This is my favorite if someone needs to calm down dramatically, or is preparing for sleep. It is a ratio of 1-second inhale to 2-second exhales, and is designed for stimulation of the vagus nerve and a strong transition to a rest and digest state in your body. I usually range between 4:8 and 5:10, but initially, I would use 3:6 very effectively to transition to sleep. Like the 5-second meditation, the focus is on the breath count and observing the breath go deep into the belly. Remember, you are only trying to count, monitor. You are not trying to pass judgment. Either of these meditations can be a great way to relax.

The last breathing meditation tip is to get you into a relaxed and peaceful mental state quickly. I was taught this by an 80-year-old yogi who travels around teaching meditation. I wouldn't tell you this if I had not experienced it myself and witnessed other people have a similar experience with this technique, since I don't have any data or studies to back up this theory. It is subtle but powerful. When you close your eyes, you start the meditation and focus your eyes upwards to the top of your forehead. So yes, with your eyes closed, gaze up at a 45-degree angle and try the 5-second breathing meditation. Enjoy!

Chapter 6
Time To Practice
Step-by-Step Guide to Effective Breathing

Breathing to the body is what electricity is to a house - without it, everything else grinds to a halt. Like electricity, breathing can be modulated and adjusted according to our needs. In this chapter, we'll explore how mastering the art of breath control can add some spark to your life.

I designed Baseline Breathing as the foundation for optimal functional breathing. Baseline Breathing protocols and exercises are suitable for all ages. They should never cause more than a slight feeling of air hunger or discomfort, and should be relaxing and conducive to an increased flow state. None of the Baseline Breathing exercises are intended to activate a fight or flight response or bring about out-of-body experiences. This was designed for better control of your autonomic system and overall health. If you are pregnant, you should always check with your doctor about any breathing exercises that may stress your body or create unease.

Overview of Breathwork Techniques

There are many advanced breathing techniques that have benefits, but I do not teach them. The Wim Hof Method and holotropic breathing are a few of the methods I don't teach or train. They have added risk to them, because of the increase in stress levels they cause, and so they cannot be used for everyone. I want to start with how much I admire Wim Hof's work and have enjoyed his sessions. I have also done many holotropic breathing sessions and had great experiences with it... but once again, it is not for everyone. These breathing styles must be done under supervision and should be approved by your doctor.

Most of the above techniques involve hyperventilation and long breath holds. Hyperventilation can dangerously reduce oxygen levels in your body, by up to 50%, and cause other serious side effects such as passing out. This is why Baseline Breathing avoids long breath holds and focuses instead on safe breathing techniques. Hyperventilation lowers your CO_2 levels, which can reduce the signal to breathe. Without CO_2 to trigger the respiratory system, people can pass out because of the O_2 levels dropping to dangerously low levels.

People have drowned in pools, and even bathtubs, while trying to push their breath hold times. Always be cautious and understand the mechanics of what you are doing. If you choose to practice long breath holds, train in a safe place and always have a spotter.

Although breath holds can be beneficial for certain individuals, it is not something recommended for individuals who are pregnant or suffering from any type of medical condition. Breath holds can trigger anxiety, which I have seen firsthand. So, medium and long breath holds are things we don't teach or train. The only long breath hold you might do, on occasion, is when you test your CO_2 tolerance.

Baseline Breathing

We recommend an equal breath hold length as your inhale or exhale rate. That means that if you breathe at 5 seconds, inhale or exhale, then a 5-second hold or pause in between is very functional. We have a slight breath hold in our box breathing exercise. If you feel more than a slight air hunger or discomfort, we recommend lowering the hold time. If you're dealing with anxiety or other health issues, we normally reduce the box breathing intervals from 5 seconds to 2-3 seconds for each side of the breath.

This is one of the factors where Baseline Breathing is different. Therefore, creating strong breathing patterns and exercises is an important factor in developing a healthy foundation for optimal health. The best way to get started is to set yourself up with a seven-day or thirty-day challenge that focuses on breathing exercises. During this challenge, you should take note of any changes you experience due to the breathing exercises. This can be a great way to track your progress and see how far you've come in just a short amount of time.

Starting off with the seven-day challenge, most people can do this with great results and no stress from such a long obligation. However, with feedback on better improvements to sleep, and optimal mental and emotional functioning, I find it much easier to commit to a 30 day challenge. They say a new habit can take 18- 254 days (2009 study, European Journal of Social Psychology). They also show it takes an average of 66 days to make a habit automatic. If you are a fan of the book Psycho Cybernetics by Dr. Maxwell Maltz, you'll know that he didn't make a study claim but did reference his own experience of a minimum of 21 days for an old mental image to dissolve and a new one take its place.

The reason I'm emphasizing these time frames is to encourage patience. You may find that you can modify certain habits faster than most, but it's entirely expected for one to occasionally lapse, even if only for a period of weeks! It's all part of the process and should not be seen as a failure.

I have encountered many things in my breathwork adventures that took me over a year to form a consistent habit of, and other things that took only 2 weeks. The great thing is that so many of the benefits of functional breathing are so obviously physically rewarding, therefore your body will have the desire to adapt to the new habits once it feels them.

Acknowledge that you have the openness to recognize what changes need to be made and possess the capability to make them. When it comes to achieving optimal breathing and overall well being, celebrate each step forward with gratitude while allowing yourself space for missteps along the way. And don't forget to enjoy your experience! Let's delve into my favorite breathing exercises.

Note: Any of the adult breathing exercises can be used with kids and vice versa.

The Perfect Breath Exercise

1. Inhale for 5-6 seconds
2. Exhale for 5-6 seconds
Repeated at an average of five-and-a-half breaths per minute.

Try this anytime you need to be in a more relaxed state. The great thing about this exercise is most people won't even know you are doing it. So it can be done anywhere. The best results are typically experienced after 5 to 10 minutes, but even a few minutes help.

Humming Sigh Through the Nose on the Exhale

Believe it or not, science has revealed that humming can release 16 times the average amount of nitric oxide compared to regular exhalation. Why is this important? Nitric oxide optimizes oxygen absorption and induces vasodilation. In addition, a slow exhale while sighing helps to relax the vagus nerve for further relaxation benefits.

1. Start with a full inhalation, with a Buddha belly breath
2. Then start the exhale hum with an
"MMMMMMMMMM...."
Try this for 5-10 rounds to discharge anger, frustration,
fear, or for a quick mental and nervous system reset.

The 4-7-8 Exercise

The 4-7-8 exercise can bring about a state of calm and peace quickly. It relaxes the parasympathetic nervous system and helps connect your body to your breath. It helps turn off the fight or flight mode and minimizes everyday thoughts that can be agitating. This exercise was also made famous by Dr. Andrew Weil. Relaxing your nervous system through this practice can be incredibly beneficial in creating a great before-bed regimen. Not only does it help you relax, but depending on the duration of the session, it's an excellent transition before your nightly reading. The instructions for this effective technique are:

Before you begin, place the tip of your tongue on the roof of your mouth just above your teeth. Keep it there. You may lie down on a flat surface or sit up with your back straight.

1. Exhale entirely through your nose, for eight seconds and
   in one large breath.

2. Close your mouth and inhale quietly and softly through your nose, for a mental count of four.
3. Hold your breath and count to seven.
4. Exhale completely through your nose, for eight seconds and in one large breath.
5. Inhale again and repeat the cycle. Do a total of four rounds, or as much as desired.

Box Breathing

This type of breath exercise helps sharpen concentration and bring about an alert but calm feeling. It facilitates getting out of the fight-or-flight mode that our body can sometimes unnecessarily go into.

The Navy Seals utilize this type of breathing for overall better performance. Remember, our Baseline Breathing way is exclusively through the nose. It is low and slow, breathing into the belly. This is typically done with a four-count breath, but if that is placing more strain on you than a slight feeling of breath hunger, lower the count by one. Then, as time goes by and you become more comfortable, up the count by one.

As always, the more you practice, the more quickly you will notice the positive health benefits. For reference, six cycles may take about two minutes. At this point, you will feel the difference. You will receive even more benefits if you have time to do five minutes or more. For the retraining process, we suggest doing this twice a day, for six weeks minimum.

1. Inhale through the nose for a four-second count
2. Hold for a four-second count
3. Exhale through the nose for a four-second count
4. Hold for a four-second count. Repeat for five to ten minutes.

Abdominal Breathing

The third and final exercise is simple and effective. It can be done anywhere that you can lie down and have a book or a light weight (2-10 lbs) handy. The purpose of this exercise is to activate abdominal breathing by creating muscle memory to breathe through your belly. So, just as before, the Baseline Breathing way is done exclusively through the nose. Your breath is low, slow, and deep in the belly.

1. Lie on the floor, with a small pillow under your head
2. Bend the knees like you would if you were doing crunches (note: we are not doing crunches!)
3. Place a book or light weight on your belly button
4. Focus on breathing through your belly
5. Breathe in, and guide the book upwards
6. Breath out, and guide the book downwards
7. Focus on having little to no chest movement; the only movement should be in your abdomen

Continue this exercise for three to five minutes. Repeat daily for six weeks.

Nasal Breathing Walks

Nasal breathing is only a 10-15 minute walk. This sounds simple, and it is. It is also one of my most favorite tools, both for myself and others. The feedback can be hilarious when you ask a partner or child for a silent, nasal breathing only walk... but it works! Usually, the other walkers will find it transformative as well.

If you are walking by yourself, don't be tempted to start talking on the phone, just focus on nasal breathing for 15 minutes of a comfortably paced walk. If you ask someone else on your walk, that is where it can become hilarious. We usually talk when we walk, but now it's time to do it in silence. When you're done with your 15 minutes, feel free to speak and breathe normally. This has been an excellent exercise for so many people dealing with things from everyday issues to severe traumas. Breathe exclusively through your nose into your belly with a slow relaxed inhale and slow relaxed exhale.

Enjoy a nice follow-your-nose quiet walk!

Brain Reset Button Breathing

This is the quickest way to a mental or physical state change. It must be done sitting down and in a safe space. It must not be done while driving. Consult your doctor if pregnant.

I have seen people pass out when they continue this practice for long periods. This is a short version of a practice known as 'fire breathing' and similar to some of the Wim Hof Method techniques, but more compact and faster.

Triple 3 Breath, or Mini Fire Breathing

This exercise involves taking 9 total breaths, with all of those breaths being deep and active. All breaths in and out can be taken through the mouth or nose (nasal preferred, but try both for this exercise).

1. 3 normal speed
2. 3 double speed
3. 3 triple speed
4. Then hold for 10 seconds, or slowly exhale for 10 seconds

Normally one cycle of the breath will give you a fast state change. Then you can go back to your normal, nasal only breathing. This breathing exercise can be repeated, but if you start to feel lightheaded take a break.

5 Kids Breathing Exercises

I always recommend that kids do breathwork with their parents. Safety and understanding are of the utmost importance. They will always get more out of breathwork when they see it, and when the importance of it is explained by someone they trust and love. I also want everyone to be able to self-regulate as much as possible, but as parents or partners, it is just as essential to co-regulate. When we co-regulate—do breathwork together—we create a stronger bond and understanding that we all share personal power and responsibility for our physical and mental health.

It is essential for parents to actively demonstrate proper breathing and exercises, rather than just passively teaching them to their children. Children learn best through observation and imitation, and by seeing the functional breathing of their parents, they can internalize the lessons they are taught. The kids pick up so much visually and are constantly absorbing the behaviors of those around them.

If a parent wants to instill the value of functional breathing in their child, they should demonstrate the importance of using breathwork. This can inspire the child to follow their lead and understand the reward that comes from putting in the effort.

To ensure the children experience a positive and long-lasting reaction, it's essential to make them feel comfortable. Therefore, they can practice breathing exercises in many positions that guarantee good posture without causing any unnecessary stress; some of these include cross-legged, sitting on a chair, or even lying flat on their back. Additionally, you could try other positions such as sitting on your heels or back-to-back.

I teach breathwork by using back-to-back and mirroring approaches with children. I recommend breathing exercises for kids be only 2-5 minutes long at first, and then ask if they would like to go longer after that time is up. Kids often enjoy breathing so much, they usually ask for another round. Use the feedback from the children to adjust to their needs or goals.

All the same rules apply here: breathe exclusively through the nose, deep into the diaphragm, with a very relaxed rate for the inhale and exhale.

Back-to-Back Breathing

Sit back-to-back on the floor, in a cross-legged position. Take a moment to ensure your backs are straight and comfortable, and you are touching each other. Place your hand comfortably on your legs. Start a count when you are both ready. Use a three or four-second count for the inhale and exhale. Keep your focus on the rhythm of each other's breathing.

The back-to-back breathing exercises can be adjusted for desired results, but their primary purpose is to increase the child's engagement with their parent. You can use the back-to-back approach with most breathing exercises.

Deep Belly Breathing

Start with one hand on the stomach, and the other on the chest. The focus is on deep diaphragmatic breathing. I use the Buddha belly image as an example of a full belly on all sides, opening the lungs, but kids can respond even more to the expanding balloon example.

The hand on the belly should be moving mostly, and the hand on the chest moving minimally. Start a count when you are both ready. Use a 3 or 4-second count for the inhale and exhale. Keep your focus on the rhythm of each other's breathing.

Bee Breathing

Get in a comfortable position and take deep belly breaths through the nose. Keep the mouth closed, exhale slowly, and make a long "MMMMM" sound. The "MMMMM" sounds can be playful, like a bee flying in the garden. Keeping the mouth closed, repeat deep belly breathing and slow buzzing exhales. Continue breathing like this for 2 minutes, or for as long as it is enjoyable. You can also make a train or ocean liner whistle sound. It is a fun and comfortable exercise that most kids respond to immediately.

Extended Exhale

All breathing is done with the mouth closed and through the nose. If they are having challenges with exhaling through their nose, they can use their mouth with pursed lips. Inhale deeply, for 3 to 5 seconds, and then exhale slowly for twice as long. For example, a 4-second inhale should be followed by an 8-second exhale. Repeat for a minute or two.

Cobra Breath

Start on your belly, and place your hands next to your shoulders. Press into your hands, lifting your head and shoulders off the ground. Take a deep belly breath through the nose for 3 seconds, then exhale for 3 seconds. Stay with this breath for a few breaths, or for as long as it is comfortable.

Parting Words

I n conclusion, the practice of breathwork is a powerful tool for enhancing overall health and wellbeing. Through intentional manipulation of our breath, we can cultivate a deeper sense of self-awareness, reduce stress and anxiety, improve physical health, and connect more authentically with our innermost selves.

Throughout this book, we have explored various techniques and approaches to breathwork, including diaphragmatic breathing, box breathing, and many more approaches suitable for kids. We have also delved into the scientific research supporting the benefits of breathwork, which includes improved focus, clarity, and immune system function.

It is my hope that readers of this book are now equipped with the necessary tools and information to incorporate optimal breathwork techniques into their daily lives. Whether you are looking to reduce stress and anxiety, improve your physical health, or deepen your spiritual practice, breathwork can help you achieve your goals. The rewards of this practice emerge most fully when it is just that - a practice. That means doing it consistently. While there are many short term benefits, the long term benefits come with patience. The key is to find the right practices that are both enjoyable and effective for you.

We encourage you to continue your exploration of breathwork from here and to make it a regular part of your self-care routine. By prioritizing your breath, and taking intentional steps toward optimal wellbeing, you are embarking on a journey to a happier, healthier, and more fulfilling life.

Bon Voyage!